Words of Jesus

and

His Early Followers

Compiled by: Catherine Martinsson
Design: Nicole Antonia

© 2023 Cascade Publishing.
All Rights Reserved.
Printed in China.

ISBN: 978-1-63264-100-7
www.cascadepublishing.com
Shop: www.mangatabooks.com

All Scripture quotations are taken from the following sources:
King James Version (KJV), Public Domain.
The New King James Version® (NKJV®). Copyright © 1982 by Thomas Nelson, Inc. Used by permission. All rights reserved.
The Holy Bible, New International Version® (NIV®). Copyright © 1973, 1978, 1984, 2011 by Biblica, Inc. All rights reserved worldwide. Used by permission.
The Holy Bible, English Standard Version® (ESV®) Copyright © 2001 by Crossway, a publishing ministry of Good News Publishers. All rights reserved.

JANUARY

1

For I am persuaded that neither death nor life, nor angels nor principalities nor powers, nor things present nor things to come, nor height nor depth, nor any other created thing, shall be able to separate us from the love of God which is in Christ Jesus our Lord.
— Romans 8:38, 39 (NKJ)

Desert Canyon, Israel

2 JANUARY

Dead Sea and Masada National Park, Israel

Fight the good fight of the faith. Take hold of the eternal life to which you were called when you made your good confession in the presence of many witnesses.
— I Timothy 6:12 (NIV)

3 JANUARY

Almond Garden, Mount Tabor, Israel

For you were bought with a price. So glorify God in your body.
— I Corinthians 6:20 (ESV)

4 JANUARY

Ancient Roman copper coins

Are not five sparrows sold for two copper coins? And not one of them is forgotten before God. But the very hairs of your head are all numbered. Do not fear therefore; you are of more value than many sparrows.
— Luke 12: 6, 7 (NKJ)

5 JANUARY

Asphodel flowers, Negev desert, Israel.

Whoever calls on the name of the LORD shall be saved.

— *Acts 2:21 (NKJ)*

6 JANUARY

Mount Sinai, Egypt

Knowledge puffs up, but love builds up.

— I Corinthians 8:1 (ESV)

7 JANUARY

Turkish cuisine

You shall receive power when the Holy Spirit has come upon you; and you shall be witnesses to Me in Jerusalem, and in all Judea and Samaria, and to the end of the earth. — *Acts 1:8 (NKJ)*

8 JANUARY

The Church of the Nativity, Bethlehem, Palestine

God demonstrates His own love toward us, in that while we were still sinners, Christ died for us.

— Romans 5:8 (NKJ)

9 JANUARY

No temptation has overtaken you that is not common to man. God is faithful, and he will not let you be tempted beyond your ability, but with the temptation He will also provide the way of escape, that you may be able to endure it.
— I Corinthians 10:13 (ESV)

Ein-Avdat Canyon, Negev Desert, Israel

10 JANUARY

Black Canyon, Israel

Except a man be born again, he cannot see the kingdom of God.
— John 3:3 (KJ)

11 JANUARY

Ancient water well

God did not give us a spirit of timidity, but a spirit of power, of love and of self-discipline.

— II Timothy 1:7 (NIV)

12 JANUARY

Dead Sea Coastline

I say to you that likewise there will be more joy in heaven over one sinner who repents than over ninety-nine just persons who need no repentance.

— *Luke 15:7 (NKJ)*

13 JANUARY

Memorial cross, The Colosseum, Rome, Italy

If I speak in the tongues of men and of angels, but have not love, I am a noisy gong or a clanging cymbal.

— I Corinthians 13:1 (ESV)

14 JANUARY

Caravan, Sahara Desert

Blessed are they which are persecuted for righteousness' sake: for theirs is the kingdom of heaven.

— Matthew 5:10 (KJ)

15 JANUARY

Church of the Good Shepherd, Lake Tekapo, New Zealand

There is therefore now no condemnation to those who are in Christ Jesus, who do not walk according to the flesh, but according to the Spirit.

— Romans 8:1 (NKJ)

16 JANUARY

Israeli falafel

Let your reasonableness be known to everyone. The Lord is at hand.
— *Philippians 4:5 (ESV)*

17 JANUARY

For the word of God is living and active. Sharper than any double-edged sword, it penetrates even to dividing soul and spirit, joints and marrow; it judges the thoughts and attitudes of the heart.
— *Hebrews 4:12 (NIV)*

Oil Lamp with The Ten Commandments

18 JANUARY

Mount Gilboa, Israel

He that is faithful in that which is least is faithful also in much: and he that is unjust in the least is unjust also in much.

— Luke 16:10 (KJ)

19 JANUARY

Ibexe, Negev Desert, Israel

Be kindly affectionate to one another with brotherly love, in honor giving preference to one another.

— Romans 12:10 (NKJ)

20 JANUARY

Sinai Peninsula and the Red Sea, Egypt

The Lord is faithful. He will establish you and guard you against the evil one.

— II Thessalonians 3:3 (ESV)

21 JANUARY

Negev Desert, Israel

I write these things to you who believe in the name of the Son of God so that you may know that you have eternal life.

— I John 5:13 (NIV)

22 JANUARY

Montazah Palace Alexandria, Egypt

Without faith it is impossible to please God, because anyone who comes to Him must believe that He exists and that He rewards those who earnestly seek Him.
— *Hebrews 11:6 (NIV)*

23 JANUARY

Palestine Sunbird

My God will supply every need of yours according to His riches in glory in Christ Jesus.

— Philippians 4:19 (ESV)

24 JANUARY

The Citadel of Qaitbay, Alexandria, Egypt

Make every effort to live in peace with all men and to be holy; without holiness no one will see the Lord.

— Hebrews 12:14 (NIV)

25 JANUARY

When ye stand praying, forgive, if ye have ought against any; that your Father also which is in heaven may forgive you your trespasses. But if ye do not forgive, neither will your Father which is in heaven forgive your trespasses.

— *Mark 11:25, 26 (KJ)*

Bell tower, Jerusalem, Israel

26 JANUARY

Red Sea, Eilat, Israel

Now he who plants and he who waters are one, and each one will receive his own reward according to his own labor.

— I Corinthians 3:8 (NKJ)

27 JANUARY

Church of All Nations, Mount of Olives, Jerusalem, Israel

Let the peace of Christ rule in your hearts, to which indeed you were called in one body. And be thankful.

— *Colossians 3:15 (ESV)*

28 JANUARY

Sinai Rosefinch, Egypt

If anyone serves Me, him My Father will honor.

— John 12:26 (NKJ)

29 JANUARY

Olive trees, Mt. Tabor, Israel

There is great gain in godliness with contentment.

— I Timothy 6:6 (ESV)

30 JANUARY

Ein Gedi National Park, Israel

Every good and perfect gift is from above, coming down from the Father of the heavenly lights, who does not change like shifting shadows.
— *James 1:17 (NIV)*

31 JANUARY

Jezreel Valley, Israel

A new commandment I give unto you, that ye love one another; as I have loved you, that ye also love one another.

— John 13:34 (KJ)

1 FEBRUARY

Tripoli, Lebanon

No man can serve two masters: for either he will hate the one, and love the other: or else he will hold to the one, and despise the other.
— *Matthew 6:24 (KJ)*

2 FEBRUARY

Old City, Jerusalem, Israel

Not that we are sufficient in ourselves to claim anything as coming from us, but our sufficiency is from God.

— *II Corinthians 3:5 (ESV)*

3 FEBRUARY

Judean desert

We have this treasure in jars of clay, to show that the surpassing power belongs to God and not to us.

— II Corinthians 4:7 (ESV)

4 FEBRUARY

Golan Heights, Israel

Humble yourselves, therefore, under God's mighty hand, that He may lift you up in due time.

— I Peter 5: 6 (NIV)

5 FEBRUARY

Cathedral of St Paul, Minnesota, USA

Love bears all things, believes all things, hopes all things, endures all things.

— I Corinthians 13:7 (ESV)

6 FEBRUARY

Caesarea National Park, Israel

Many prophets and righteous men desired to see what you see, and did not see it, and to hear what you hear, and did not hear it.

— Matthew 13:17 (NKJ)

7 FEBRUARY

Wooden Felucca, Nile River, Egypt

There remains, then, a Sabbath-rest for the people of God; for anyone who enters God's rest also rests from his own work, just as God did from His. — *Hebrews 4:9, 10 (NIV)*

8 FEBRUARY

Old City, Jerusalem, Israel

Thou shalt love the Lord thy God with all thy heart, and with all thy soul, and with all thy strength, and with all thy mind; and thy neighbor as thyself.
— Luke 10:27 (KJ)

9 FEBRUARY

I have fought the good fight, I have finished the race, I have kept the faith. Now there is in store for me the crown of righteousness, which the Lord, the righteous Judge, will award to me on that day--and not only to me, but also to all who have longed for his appearing.

— *II Timothy 4:7, 8 (NIV)*

Marzamemi, Sicily, Italy

10 FEBRUARY

Red Sea, Egypt

The kingdom of God does not come with observation; nor will they say, 'See here!' or 'See there!' For indeed, the kingdom of God is within you.

— *Luke 17: 20, 21 (NKJ)*

11 FEBRUARY

Nile River, Luxor, Egypt

Give thanks in all circumstances; for this is the will of God in Christ Jesus for you.

— I Thessalonians 5:18 (ESV)

12 FEBRUARY

Spice shop, open market, Israel

Seek ye first the kingdom of God, and his righteousness; and all these things shall be added unto you.

— Matthew 6:33 (KJ)

13 FEBRUARY

Sand Cat (Felis margarita)

We brought nothing into the world, and we can take nothing out of it. But if we have food and clothing, we will be content with that.

— I Timothy 6:7, 8 (NIV)

14 FEBRUARY

The Cathedral of Syracuse, Sicily, Italy

He saved us, not because of righteous things we had done, but because of his mercy. He saved us through the washing of rebirth and renewal by the Holy Spirit.

— Titus 3:5 (NIV)

15 FEBRUARY

Matzoh, unleavened bread

I am the bread of life: he that cometh to me shall never hunger; and he that believeth on me shall never thirst.

— John 6:35 (KJ)

16 FEBRUARY

Wadi Rum, Jordan

Let each of you look not only to his own interests, but also to the interests of others.

— *Philippians 2:4 (ESV)*

17 FEBRUARY

Consider the lilies, how they grow: they neither toil nor spin; and yet I say to you, even Solomon in all his glory was not arrayed like one of these. If then God so clothes the grass, which today is in the field and tomorrow is thrown into the oven, how much more will He clothe you, O you of little faith?
— Luke 12:27, 28 (NKJ)

The Siq, Petra, Jordan

18 FEBRUARY

Crete, Greece

How hardly shall they that have riches enter into the kingdom of God? It is easier for a camel to go through the eye of a needle, than for a rich man to enter into the kingdom of God. — *Luke 18:24, 25 (KJ)*

19 FEBRUARY

Mount Sinai, Egypt

Pray without ceasing.

— I Thessalonians 5:17 (ESV)

20 FEBRUARY

Dead Sea, Israel

No one serving as a soldier gets involved in civilian affairs--he wants to please his commanding officer.

— II Timothy 2:4 (NIV)

21 FEBRUARY

Cranes, Hula Lake Reserve, Israel

He that is greatest among you shall be your servant. And whosoever shall exalt himself shall be abased; and he that shall humble himself shall be exalted.
— Matthew 23: 11,12 (KJ)

22 FEBRUARY

Rosh HaNikra, Galilee, Israel

I am come a light into the world, that whosoever believeth on me should not abide in darkness.

— John 12:46 (KJ)

23 FEBRUARY

Jewish Quarter, Old Jerusalem, Israel

The second (commandment) is this: You shall love your neighbor as yourself. There is no other commandment greater than these.

— Mark 12:31 (NKJ)

24 FEBRUARY

Crete, Greece

May the Lord make you increase and abound in love for one another and for all, as we do for you.

— I Thessalonians 3:12 (ESV)

25 FEBRUARY

That is why I am suffering as I am. Yet I am not ashamed, because I know whom I have believed, and am convinced that He is able to guard what I have entrusted to Him for that day.

— II Timothy 1:12 (NIV)

Cedar forest, Lebanon

26 FEBRUARY

Vineyard, Israel

I am the vine, you are the branches. He who abides in Me, and I in him, bears much fruit; for without Me you can do nothing.

— John 15: 5 (NKJ)

27 FEBRUARY

Elafonisi Beach, Crete, Greece

Who shall separate us from the love of Christ? Shall tribulation, or distress, or persecution, or famine, or nakedness, or peril, or sword?
— *Romans 8:35 (NKJ)*

28 FEBRUARY

Kidron Valley, Judea, Israel

With men it is impossible, but not with God: for with God all things are possible.

— Mark 10:27 (KJ)

29 FEBRUARY

Crete, Greece

If I give away all I have, and if I deliver up my body to be burned, but have not love, I gain nothing.

— I Corinthians 13:3 (ESV)

1 MARCH

The weapons of our warfare are not of the flesh but have divine power to destroy strongholds. We destroy arguments and every lofty opinion raised against the knowledge of God, and take every thought captive to obey Christ.
— *II Corinthians 10:4, 5 (ESV)*

Masada, Israel

2 MARCH

Dead Sea, Israel

Man shall not live by bread alone, but by every word that proceedeth out of the mouth of God.

— Matthew 4:4 (KJ)

3 MARCH

Budakirkja Church, Saefellsnes peninsula, Iceland

Do nothing from rivalry or conceit, but in humility count others more significant than yourselves.

— Philippians 2:3 (ESV)

4 MARCH

Bogliasco, Italy

If you abide in Me, and My words abide in you, you will ask what you desire, and it shall be done for you.

— *John 15:7 (NKJ)*

5 MARCH

Al-Khazneh ("The Treasury"), Petra, Jordan

For God so loved the world, that He gave His only begotten Son, that whosoever believeth in Him should not perish, but have everlasting life.
— John 3:16 (KJ)

6 MARCH

Metal teapots, Bedouin cafe, Petra

As we have opportunity, let us do good to everyone, and especially to those who are of the household of faith.

— Galatians 6:10 (ESV)

7 MARCH

Netanya City, Israel

We must pay more careful attention, therefore, to what we have heard, so that we do not drift away.

— *Hebrews 2:1 (NIV)*

8 MARCH

Nile River, Egypt

The harvest truly is plentiful, but the laborers are few. Therefore pray the Lord of the harvest to send out laborers into His harvest.
— *Matthew 9:37, 38 (NKJ)*

9 MARCH

So that Christ may dwell in your hearts through faith—that you, being rooted and grounded in love, may have strength to comprehend with all the saints what is the breadth and length and height and depth, and to know the love of Christ that surpasses knowledge.
— *Ephesians 3:17–19 (ESV)*

Date Palm Plantation, Jordan Valley, Israel

10 MARCH

Old Jaffa Port, Tel-Aviv, Israel

But He said to me, "My grace is sufficient for you, for my power is made perfect in weakness." Therefore I will boast all the more gladly of my weaknesses, so that the power of Christ may rest upon me.

— II Corinthians 12:9 (ESV)

11 MARCH

Dead Sea, Ein Bokek, Israel

If you abide in My word, you are My disciples indeed. You shall know the truth, and the truth shall make you free.

— *John 8:31, 32 (NKJ)*

12 MARCH

Mount Ararat and Lesser Ararat, Turkey

The kingdom of heaven is like unto a merchantman, seeking goodly pearls: who, when he had found one pearl of great price, went and sold all that he had, and bought it. — *Matthew 13:45, 46 (KJ)*

13 MARCH

Ashkelon, Israel

As long as I am in the world, I am the light of the world.
— *John 9:5 (NKJ)*

14 MARCH

Almond tree, Sataf Reserve, Jerusalem hills

Blessed are the meek: for they shall inherit the earth.
— Matthew 5:5 (KJ)

15 MARCH

Chania Lighthouse, Crete, Greece

You need to persevere so that when you have done the will of God, you will receive what he has promised.

— *Hebrews 10:36 (NIV)*

16 MARCH

Tarsus Waterfall, Turkey

The eyes of the Lord are on the righteous and his ears are attentive to their prayer, but the face of the Lord is against those who do evil.
— *I Peter 3:12 (NIV)*

17 MARCH

I therefore, a prisoner for the Lord, urge you to walk in a manner worthy of the calling to which you have been called, with all humility and gentleness, with patience, bearing with one another in love, eager to maintain the unity of the Spirit in the bond of peace.

— *Ephesians 4:1-3 (ESV)*

Ras Muhammad National Park, Red Sea, Egypt

18 MARCH

Tel Aviv-Jaffa, Israel

How great is the love the Father has lavished on us, that we should be called children of God!

— I John 3:1 (NIV)

19 MARCH

Tower of David, Jerusalem, Israel

I am the light of the world: he that followeth me shall not walk in darkness, but shall have the light of life.

— *John 8:12 (KJ)*

20 MARCH

Malta

Take heed and beware of covetousness, for one's life does not consist in the abundance of the things he possesses.

— Luke 12:15 (NKJ)

21 March

Hagia Maria Sion Abbey Church, Jerusalem, Israel

Let your speech always be gracious, seasoned with salt, so that you may know how you ought to answer each person.

— Colossians 4:6 (ESV)

22 MARCH

Alexandria Castle, Egypt

Do your best to present yourself to God as one approved, a workman who does not need to be ashamed and who correctly handles the word of truth.
— II Timothy 2:15 (NIV)

23 MARCH

Timna Park, Israel

Rejoicing in hope, patient in tribulation, continuing steadfastly in prayer.

— Romans 12:12 (NKJ)

24 MARCH

Santa Maria dell'Isola Monastery, Tropea, Italy

We do not lose heart. Though our outer self is wasting away, our inner self is being renewed day by day.

— *II Corinthians 4:16 (ESV)*

25 MARCH

The Lord Himself will descend from heaven with a cry of command, with the voice of an archangel, and with the sound of the trumpet of God. And the dead in Christ will rise first. Then we who are alive, who are left, will be caught up together with them in the clouds to meet the Lord in the air, and so we will always be with the Lord.
— *I Thessalonians 4:16, 17 (ESV)*

Nazarath, Israel

26 MARCH

Old City, Jerusalem, Israel

I am the First and the Last. I am the Living One; I was dead, and behold I am alive for ever and ever! And I hold the keys of death and Hades.
— Revelations 1:17, 18 (NIV)

27 MARCH

Baia del Silenzio, Sestri Levante, Italy

I say to you, whoever confesses Me before men, him the Son of Man also will confess before the angels of God.

— *Luke 12:8 (NKJ)*

28 MARCH

Sidon Sea Castle, Sidon, Lebanon

He who calls you is faithful; He will surely do it.
— I Thessalonians 5:24 (ESV)

29 MARCH

Hummus and ingredients

This is the confidence we have in approaching God: that if we ask anything according to His will, He hears us.

— I John 5:14 (NIV)

30 MARCH

Basilica of St. Francis of Assisi, Umbria, Italy

I am the good shepherd: the good shepherd giveth his life for the sheep.

— *John 10:11-13 (KJ)*

31 MARCH

Old City, Jerusalem, Israel

For the kingdom of God is not eating and drinking, but righteousness and peace and joy in the Holy Spirit.

— *Romans 14:17 (NKJ)*

1 APRIL

Sinai Agama

If I have prophetic powers, and understand all mysteries and all knowledge, and if I have all faith, so as to remove mountains, but have not love, I am nothing. — *I Corinthians 13:2 (ESV)*

2 APRIL

Santorini Island, Greece

For judgment I have come into this world, that those who do not see may see, and that those who see may be made blind.

— John 9:39 (NKJ)

3 APRIL

Mount Scopus, Jerusalem, Israel

If ye had faith as a grain of mustard seed, ye might say unto this sycamine tree, Be thou plucked up by the root, and be thou planted in the sea; and it should obey you.
— Luke 17:6 (KJ)

4 APRIL

Via Dolorosa-Station IX, Old City Jerusalem

Do not grow weary in doing good.

— II Thessalonians 3:13 (ESV)

5 APRIL

Netanya City, Israel

Perseverance must finish its work so that you may be mature and complete, not lacking anything.

— *James 1:4 (NIV)*

6 APRIL

Giza Plateau, Egypt

Whoever gives you a cup of water to drink in My name, because you belong to Christ, assuredly, I say to you, he will by no means lose his reward.
— *Mark 9:41 (NKJ)*

7 APRIL

Cranes, Hula Lake Reserve, Israel

Whatever you do, work heartily, as for the Lord and not for men.
— *Colossians 3:23 (ESV)*

8 APRIL

Red Sea, Sharm El Sheikh, Egypt

Let us then approach the throne of grace with confidence, so that we may receive mercy and find grace to help us in our time of need.
— Hebrews 4:16 (NIV)

9 APRIL

Which of you, intending to build a tower, does not sit down first and count the cost, whether he has enough to finish it—lest, after he has laid the foundation, and is not able to finish, all who see it begin to mock him, saying, 'This man began to build and was not able to finish'?
— *Luke 14:28-30 (NKJ)*

Isola delle Correnti, Sicily, Italy

10 APRIL

Jaffa, Israel

Whatever you do, in word or deed, do everything in the name of the Lord Jesus, giving thanks to God the Father through Him.

— *Colossians 3:17 (ESV)*

11 APRIL

Red Sea, Sharm El Sheikh, Egypt

The Lord will rescue me from every evil attack and will bring me safely to His heavenly kingdom. To Him be glory for ever and ever.
— II Timothy 4:18 (NIV)

12 APRIL

Hermon Nature Reserve, Israel

Be of the same mind toward one another. Do not set your mind on high things, but associate with the humble. Do not be wise in your own opinion.
— Romans 12:16 (NKJ)

13 APRIL

Crete, Greece

Love does not insist on its own way; it is not irritable or resentful.
— *I Corinthians 13:5 (ESV)*

14 APRIL

Black Iris, Umm Qais, Jordan

Everyone born of God overcomes the world. This is the victory that has overcome the world, even our faith.

— I John 5:4 (NIV)

15 APRIL

Dead Sea, Israel

Why are ye so fearful? How is it that ye have no faith?

— Mark 4:40 (KJ)

16 APRIL

Sant'Angelo, Ischia Island, Italy

Whatsoever ye shall ask in my name, that will I do, that the Father may be glorified in the Son.

— John 14:13 (KJ)

17 APRIL

Him who overcomes I will make a pillar in the temple of my God. Never again will he leave it. I will write on him the name of my God and the name of the city of my God, the new Jerusalem, which is coming down out of heaven from my God; and I will also write on him my new name.
— *Revelations 3:12 (NIV)*

Spring meadow, Jerusalem, Israel

18 APRIL

Marsaxlokk, Malta

A good man out of the good treasure of his heart bringeth forth that which is good; and an evil man out of the evil treasure of his heart bringeth forth that which is evil: for of the abundance of the heart his mouth speaketh.
— *Luke 6:45 (KJ)*

19 APRIL

Kalymnos, Greece

Faith comes by hearing, and hearing by the word of God.
— *Romans 10:17 (NKJ)*

20 APRIL

Celsus Library, Ephesus, Turkey

That according to the riches of His glory He may grant you to be strengthened with power through His Spirit in your inner being.

— *Ephesians 3:16 (ESV)*

21 APRIL

Bougainvillea, Judean Mountains, Israel

My dear brothers, take note of this: Everyone should be quick to listen, slow to speak and slow to become angry.

— James 1:19 (NIV)

22 APRIL

Roman Aqueduct, Ceasarea, Israel

This is the will of the Father who sent Me, that of all He has given Me I should lose nothing, but should raise it up at the last day.

— *John 6:39 (NKJ)*

23 APRIL

Myrrh

Since we are surrounded by such a great cloud of witnesses, let us throw off everything that hinders and the sin that so easily entangles, and let us run with perseverance the race marked out for us.

— *Hebrews 12:1 (NIV)*

24 APRIL

Caesarea, Israel

Let the word of Christ dwell in you richly, teaching and admonishing one another in all wisdom, singing psalms and hymns and spiritual songs, with thankfulness in your hearts to God. — *Colossians 3:16 (ESV)*

25 APRIL

Love your enemies, bless them that curse you, do good to them that hate you, and pray for them which despitefully use you, and persecute you; That ye may be the children of your Father which is in heaven: for He maketh His sun to rise on the evil and on the good, and sendeth rain on the just and on the unjust.
— *Matthew 5:44, 45 (KJ)*

Nazareth, Israel

26 APRIL

Tiberias, Galilee, Israel

Owe no one anything except to love one another, for he who loves another has fulfilled the law.

— Romans 13:8 (NKJ)

27 APRIL

Old Jaffa City, Tel Aviv, Israel

Christ has set us free; stand firm therefore, and do not submit again to a yoke of slavery.

— Galatians 5:1 (ESV)

28 APRIL

Red Sea, Marsa Alam, Egypt

If ye shall ask anything in my name, I will do it.

— John 14:14 (KJ)

29 APRIL

Solanto Village, Sicily, Italy

But you, when you pray, go into your room, and when you have shut your door, pray to your Father who is in the secret place; and your Father who sees in secret will reward you openly. — *Matthew 6:6 (NKJ)*

30 APRIL

Rüppell's fox, Wadi Rum, Jordan

We do not have a high priest who is unable to sympathize with our weaknesses, but we have one who has been tempted in every way, just as we are--yet was without sin.
— *Hebrews 4:15 (NIV)*

1 MAY

Put on then, as God's chosen ones, holy and beloved, compassionate hearts, kindness, humility, meekness, and patience, bearing with one another and, if one has a complaint against another, forgiving each other; as the Lord has forgiven you, so you also must forgive.
— *Colossians 3:12,13 (ESV)*

Abbey of the Dormition, Jerusalem, Israel

2 MAY

Comino Island, Malta

Blessed are ye, when men shall revile you, and persecute you, and shall say all manner of evil against you falsely, for my sake.

— Matthew 5:11 (KJ)

3 MAY

Ajloun, Jordan

He has given us his very great and precious promises, so that through them you may participate in the divine nature and escape the corruption in the world caused by evil desires.
— II Peter 1:4 (NIV)

4 MAY

Akamas Peninsula National Park, Cyprus

The whole law is fulfilled in one word: You shall love your neighbor as yourself.

— Galatians 5:14 (ESV)

5 MAY

East Wall, Jerusalem, Israel

Dear children, let us not love with words or tongue but with actions and in truth.

— I John 3:18 (NIV)

6 MAY

Rosh HaNikra, Galilee, Israel

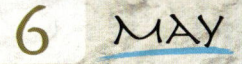

Greater love hath no man than this, that a man lay down his life for his friends.

— *John 15:13 (KJ)*

7 MAY

Al-Khazneh ("The Treasury"), Petra, Jordan

If ye love me keep my commandments.

— John 14:15 (KJ)

8 MAY

Saint Paul's Church, Tarsus, Turkey

For whoever calls on the name of the LORD shall be saved.
— Romans 10:13 (NKJ)

9 MAY

Now to Him who is able to do far more abundantly than all that we ask or think, according to the power at work within us, to Him be glory in the church and in Christ Jesus throughout all generations, forever and ever.

— *Ephesians 3:20, 21 (ESV)*

Red Sea, Egypt

10 MAY

Church of St. George, Lalibela, Ethiopia

Love is patient and kind; love does not envy or boast; it is not arrogant or rude.

— *I Corinthians 13:4 (ESV)*

11 MAY

Galshanim beach, Haifa, Israel

Endure hardship with us like a good soldier of Christ Jesus.
— II Timothy 2:3 (NIV)

12 MAY

Avshalom Stalactites Cave, Soreq, Israel

The kingdom of heaven is like treasure hidden in a field which a man found and hid; and for joy over it he goes and sells all that he has and buys that field. — *Matthew 13:44 (NKJ)*

13 MAY

Navagio Beach, Zakynthos island, Greece

Above all these put on love, which binds everything together in perfect harmony.

— *Colossians 3:14 (ESV)*

14 MAY

Old City, Jerusalem, Israel

Faith is being sure of what we hope for and certain of what we do not see.

— *Hebrews 11:1 (NIV)*

15 MAY

Paphos, Cyprus

I am the resurrection and the life. He who believes in Me, though he may die, he shall live. And whoever lives and believes in Me shall never die.
— *John 11:25, 26 (NKJ)*

16 MAY

Church of the Holy Apostles, Capernaum, Israel

Let not your heart be troubled, neither let it be afraid.
— John 14:27 (KJ)

17 MAY

What man is there of you, whom if his son ask bread, will he give him a stone? Or if he asks a fish, will he give him a serpent? If ye then, being evil, know how to give good gifts unto your children, how much more shall your Father which is in heaven give good things to them that ask Him?
— Matthew 7:9 - 11 (KJ)

Biete Abba Libanos, Lalibela, Ethiopia

18 MAY

St. Peter's Basilica, Vatican City

Rejoice always.

— I Thessalonians 5:16 (ESV)

19 MAY

Negev Desert, Israel

Eye has not seen, nor ear heard, nor have entered into the heart of man the things which God has prepared for those who love Him.

— *I Corinthians 2:9 (NKJ)*

20 MAY

Oia, Santorini Island, Greece

The servant is not greater than his lord: neither he that is sent greater than he that sent him. If ye know these things, happy are ye if ye do them.
— John 13:16, 17 (KJ)

21 MAY

Sailboat, Red Sea, Egypt

Let the one who boasts, boast in the Lord.

— II Corinthians 10:17 (ESV)

22 MAY

Biblical Tamar Park, Hazeva, Israel

If we are faithless, He will remain faithful, for He cannot disown himself.

— II Timothy 2:13 (NIV)

23 May

Palestinian Olives

He who did not spare His own Son, but delivered Him up for us all, how shall He not with Him also freely give us all things?

— Romans 8:32 (NKJ)

24 MAY

Boswellia (Frankincense) Tree

I am with you always, even to the end of the age.

— *Matthew 28:20 (NKJ)*

25 MAY

The Lord's servant must not quarrel; instead, he must be kind to everyone, able to teach, not resentful. Those who oppose him he must gently instruct, in the hope that God will grant them repentance leading them to a knowledge of the truth.
— II Timothy 2:24, 25 (NIV)

Jericho, Palestine

26 MAY

Mount of Olives, Jerusalem, Israel

He himself is our peace, who has made us both one and has broken down in His flesh the dividing wall of hostility.

— *Ephesians 2:14 (ESV)*

27 MAY

Sharm-el-sheikh, Egypt

Let us hold unswervingly to the hope we profess, for He who promised is faithful.

— Hebrews 10:23 (NIV)

28 MAY

Popeye Village, Malta

Do you not know that you are the temple of God and that the Spirit of God dwells in you?

— I Corinthians 3:16 (NKJ)

29 MAY

Birgu, Malta

Father, if it be possible, if thou be willing, remove this cup from me: nevertheless not my will, but thine, be done.

— Mark 14:36 (KJ)

30 MAY

Mount Sinai, Egypt

The fruit of the Spirit is love, joy, peace, patience, kindness, goodness, faithfulness, gentleness, self-control; against such things there is no law.
— *Galatians 5:22, 23 (ESV)*

31 MAY

Santorini, Greece

Blessed is the man who perseveres under trial, because when he has stood the test, he will receive the crown of life that God has promised to those who love Him.
— *James 1:12 (NIV)*

1 JUNE

Jerash, Jordan

These things I have spoken unto you, that in me ye might have peace. In the world ye shall have tribulation: but be of good cheer; I have overcome the world.
— *John 16:33 (KJ)*

2 JUNE

Wadi Rum, Jordan

Rejoice with those who rejoice, and weep with those who weep.
— Romans 12:15 (NKJ)

3 JUNE

Synagogue, Capernaum, Israel

Love does not rejoice at wrongdoing, but rejoices with the truth.
— *I Corinthians 13:6 (ESV)*

4 JUNE

Roman amphitheater, Aspendos, Turkey

Preach the Word; be prepared in season and out of season; correct, rebuke and encourage--with great patience and careful instruction.
— *II Timothy 4:2 (NIV)*

5 JUNE

Giza Plateau, Egypt

I am the true vine, and My Father is the vinedresser. Every branch in Me that does not bear fruit He takes away; and every branch that bears fruit He prunes, that it may bear more fruit. — *John 15:1, 2 (NKJ)*

6 JUNE

Dead Sea, Israel

I can do all things through Him who strengthens me.
— *Philippians 4:13 (ESV)*

7 JUNE

Basilica of Annunciation, Nazareth, Israel

Not lagging in diligence, fervent in spirit, serving the Lord.
— *Romans 12:11 (NKJ)*

8 JUNE

Blue Lagoon, Egypt

Who comforts us in all our affliction, so that we may be able to comfort those who are in any affliction, with the comfort with which we ourselves are comforted by God. — *II Corinthians 1:4 (ESV)*

9 JUNE

To what shall we liken the kingdom of God? Or with what parable shall we picture it? It is like a mustard seed which, when it is sown on the ground, is smaller than all the seeds on earth; but when it is sown, it grows up and becomes greater than all herbs, and shoots out large branches, so that the birds of the air may nest under its shade.

— *Mark 4: 30-32 (NKJ)*

Old City wall, Jerusalem, Israel

10 JUNE

Paphos, Cyprus

Do not throw away your confidence; it will be richly rewarded.
— *Hebrews 10:35 (NIV)*

11 JUNE

Sea of Galilee, Tiberias, Israel

For the Son of man is come to seek and to save that which was lost.
— *Luke 19:10 (KJ)*

12 JUNE

Statue of Apostle Peter, Capernaum, Israel

Not that I am speaking of being in need, for I have learned in whatever situation I am to be content.

— *Philippians 4:11 (ESV)*

13 JUNE

Wild lily, Hof Dor, Israel

You did not choose Me, but I chose you and appointed you that you should go and bear fruit, and that your fruit should remain, that whatever you ask the Father in My name He may give you. — *John 15:16 (NKJ)*

14 JUNE

Garden Tomb, Jerusalem, Israel

For God is not a God of confusion but of peace.
— I Corinthians 14:33 (ESV)

15 JUNE

Dome of the Ascension, Mount of Olives, Jerusalem

Humble yourselves before the Lord, and He will lift you up.
— James 4:10 (NIV)

16 JUNE

Garden Tomb, Jerusalem, Israel

Dear friends, if our hearts do not condemn us, we have confidence before God and receive from Him anything we ask, because we obey His commands and do what pleases Him. — *I John 3:21, 22 (NIV)*

17 JUNE

If any of you lacks wisdom, he should ask God, who gives generously to all without finding fault, and it will be given to him. But when he asks, he must believe and not doubt, because he who doubts is like a wave of the sea, blown and tossed by the wind.

— *James 1:5, 6 (NIV)*

Crusader Fortress, Caesarea, Israel

18 JUNE

Judean Desert

As you received Christ Jesus the Lord, so walk in Him, rooted and built up in Him and established in the faith, just as you were taught, abounding in thanksgiving.

— Colossians 2:6, 7 (ESV)

19 JUNE

Tower of David, Jerusalem, Israel

If it is possible, as much as depends on you, live peaceably with all men.

— Romans 12:18 (NKJ)

20 June

Ein Gedi Nature Reserve and National Park, Israel

For now we see in a mirror dimly, but then face to face. Now I know in part; then I shall know fully, even as I have been fully known.
— I Corinthians 13:12 (ESV)

21 JUNE

Qumran, Kalya, Palestine

Let us consider how we may spur one another on toward love and good deeds.

— Hebrews 10:24 (NIV)

22 JUNE

Mount Sinai, Egypt

The peace of God, which surpasses all understanding, will guard your hearts and your minds in Christ Jesus.

— *Philippians 4:7 (ESV)*

23 JUNE

Sardinia, Italy

By this shall all men know that ye are my disciples, if ye have love one to another.

— John 13:35 (KJ)

24 JUNE

Caesarea Maritima, Israel

He that is without sin among you, let him first cast a stone.
— John 8:7 (KJ)

25 JUNE

What man of you, having a hundred sheep, if he loses one of them, does not leave the ninety-nine in the wilderness, and go after the one which is lost until he finds it? Likewise there will be more joy in heaven over one sinner who repents than over ninety-nine just persons who need no repentance.

— Luke 15:4,7 (NKJ)

Old City, Jerusalem, Israel

26 JUNE

Myrrh, Gold, and Frankincense

Confess your sins to each other and pray for each other so that you may be healed. The prayer of a righteous man is powerful and effective.

— James 5:16 (NIV)

27 JUNE

Tel Dor, Israel

Giving thanks to the Father, who has qualified you to share in the inheritance of the saints in light.

— Colossians 1:12 (ESV)

28 JUNE

Biete Qeddus Mercoreus, Lalibela, Ethiopia

Go therefore and make disciples of all the nations, baptizing them in the name of the Father and of the Son and of the Holy Spirit.
— Matthew 28:19 (NKJ)

29 JUNE

Date stalks, Jericho, Palestine

This is His command: to believe in the name of His Son, Jesus Christ, and to love one another as He commanded us.

— I John 3:23 (NIV)

30 JUNE

These have come so that your faith—of greater worth than gold, which perishes even though refined by fire--may be proved genuine and may result in praise, glory and honor when Jesus Christ is revealed.

— I Peter 1:7 (NIV)

Rosh HaNikra, Galilee, Israel

1 JULY

Passover foods

By this My Father is glorified, that you bear much fruit; so you will be My disciples.

— John 15:8 (NKJ)

Church of John the Baptist, Al-Maghtas, Jordan

2 JULY

Keep on loving each other as brothers. Do not forget to entertain strangers, for by so doing some people have entertained angels without knowing it. — *Hebrews 13:1, 2 (NIV)*

3 JULY

Have faith in God. For assuredly, I say to you, whoever says to this mountain, be removed and be cast into the sea, and does not doubt in his heart, but believes that those things he says will be done, he will have whatever he says.
— *Mark 11:22, 23 (NKJ)*

Figs, Carmel Market, Tel Aviv

Positano, Amalfi Coast, Italy

4 JULY

Those who obey His commands live in Him, and He in them. And this is how we know that He lives in us: We know it by the Spirit He gave us.
— I John 3:24 (NIV)

Mont Saint Michel Abbey, Normandy, France   **5**   JULY

Love never ends. As for prophecies, they will pass away; as for tongues, they will cease; as for knowledge, it will pass away.

— *I Corinthians 13:8 (ESV)*

Olive Grove, Greece

6 JULY

God is not the God of the dead, but the God of the living.
— Matthew 22:32 (KJ)

Ayia Napa, Cyprus

7 JULY

If anyone loves Me, he will keep My word; and My Father will love him, and We will come to him and make Our home with him.

— John 14:23 (NKJ)

8 JULY

For you know the grace of our Lord Jesus Christ, that though He was rich, yet for your sake He became poor, so that you by His poverty might become rich.
— II Corinthians 8:9 (ESV)

Beach near Ashkelon, Israel

Old city Jerusalem, Israel **9 JULY**

Blessed be the God and Father of our Lord Jesus Christ, who has blessed us in Christ with every spiritual blessing in the heavenly places.
— Ephesians 1:3 (ESV)

Cranes, Hula Nature Reserve, Israel

10 JULY

Keep your lives free from the love of money and be content with what you have, because God has said, "Never will I leave you; never will I forsake you."
— Hebrews 13:5 (NIV)

Temple platform, Jerusalem, Israel

11 JULY

Let not your heart be troubled: ye believe in God, believe also in me.
— *John 14:1 (KJ)*

Dead Sea, Ein Bokek, Israel

12 JULY

Set your minds on things that are above, not on things that are on earth.

— *Colossians 3:2 (ESV)*

Chapel Senhor da Pedra, Miramar Beach, Portugal — **13 JULY**

Oh, the depth of the riches both of the wisdom and knowledge of God! How unsearchable are His judgments and His ways past finding out!
— Romans 11:33 (NKJ)

Qumran Caves, Kalya, Palestine

14 JULY

He that believeth on me, the works that I do shall he do also; and greater works than these shall he do; because I go unto my Father.

— *John 14:12 (KJ)*

The Shepherds Field Chapel, Bethlehem, Palestine

15 JULY

So now faith, hope, and love abide, these three; but the greatest of these is love.

— *I Corinthians 13:13 (ESV)*

16 JULY

Finally, brothers, whatever is true, whatever is honorable, whatever is just, whatever is pure, whatever is lovely, whatever is commendable, if there is any excellence, if there is anything worthy of praise, think about these things.

— Philippians 4:8 (ESV)

Ma'amoul, cookies filled with dates, pistachios and walnuts

Donkey and colt, Old City, Jerusalem

17 JULY

Consider it pure joy, my brothers, whenever you face trials of many kinds, because you know that the testing of your faith develops perseverance.
— *James 1:2, 3 (NIV)*

Mount Arbel National park, Israel

18 JULY

Whoever seeks to save his life will lose it, and whoever loses his life will preserve it.

— Luke 17:33 (NKJ)

Ein Gedi National Park, Israel   19 JULY

If then you have been raised with Christ, seek the things that are above, where Christ is, seated at the right hand of God.

— Colossians 3:1 (ESV)

Statue of Saint Peter, Vatican City   **20** JULY

I must work the works of Him who sent Me while it is day; the night is coming when no one can work.

— John 9:4 (NKJ)

Sinai Mountains, Sharm el Sheikh, Egypt

21 JULY

Whatsoever ye shall bind on earth shall be bound in heaven: and whatsoever ye shall loose on earth shall be loosed in heaven.

— Matthew 18:18 (KJ)

Cedars of God, Bsharri, Lebanon

22 JULY

Do not be anxious about anything, but in everything by prayer and supplication with thanksgiving let your requests be made known to God.
— *Philippians 4:6 (ESV)*

Crete, Greece 23 JULY

Show proper respect to everyone: Love the brotherhood of believers, fear God, honor the king.

— I Peter 2:17 (NIV)

24 JULY

The first of all the commandments is: Hear, O Israel, the LORD our God, the LORD is one. And you shall love the LORD your God with all your heart, with all your soul, with all your mind, and with all your strength. This is the first commandment.
— *Mark 12:29, 30 (NKJ)*

Poppy Anemone, Amman, Jordan

Red Canyon, Eilat Mountains, Israel

25 JULY

This is My commandment, that you love one another as I have loved you.

— John 15:12 (NKJ)

Haifa, Israel

26 JULY

Be kind to one another, tenderhearted, forgiving one another, as God in Christ forgave you.

— *Ephesians 4:32 (ESV)*

Khubz, Arabic Bread

27 JULY

Men always ought to pray and not lose heart.

— Luke 18:1 (NKJ)

Gulf of Aqaba, Eilat City, Israel

28 JULY

For the sake of Christ, then, I am content with weaknesses, insults, hardships, persecutions, and calamities. For when I am weak, then I am strong.
— II Corinthians 12:10 (ESV)

Selesian Church, Nazareth, Israel — **29** JULY

Blessed are the poor in spirit: for theirs is the kingdom of heaven.
— *Matthew 5:3 (KJ)*

Mary Magdalene Convent, Mount of Olives, Jerusalem — **30** JULY

Say not there are yet four months, and then cometh harvest? Behold, I say unto you, Lift up your eyes, and look on the fields; for they are white already to harvest.
— *John 4:35 (KJ)*

City wall, Jerusalem, Israel

31 JULY

When I was a child, I spoke like a child, I thought like a child, I reasoned like a child. When I became a man, I gave up childish ways.
— I Corinthians 13:11 (ESV)

Vineyard, Kfar Tabor, Israel

1 AUGUST

In my Father's house are many mansions: if it were not so, I would have told you.

— John 14:2 (KJ)

Fortezza Aragonese, Isola di Capo Rizzuto, Italy

2 AUGUST

Indeed there are last who will be first, and there are first who will be last.

— *Luke 13:30 (NKJ)*

Bcharre, Lebanon

3 AUGUST

We are afflicted in every way, but not crushed; perplexed, but not driven to despair; persecuted, but not forsaken; struck down, but not destroyed; — *II Corinthians 4:8, 9 (ESV)*

Arbel agriculture valley, Sea of Galilee, Israel

4 AUGUST

All men are like grass, and all their glory is like the flowers of the field; the grass withers and the flowers fall, but the word of the Lord stands forever.
— I Peter 1:24, 25 (NIV)

Almond trees, Sataf Reserve, Jerusalem

5 AUGUST

The Comforter, which is the Holy Ghost, whom the Father will send in my name, He shall teach you all things, and bring all things to your remembrance, whatsoever I have said unto you. — *John 14:26 (KJ)*

Nafpaktos Port, Gulf of Corinth, Greece

6 AUGUST

Rejoice in the Lord always; again I will say, Rejoice.

— *Philippians 4:4 (ESV)*

Church of the Multiplication, Tabgha, Israel — **7 AUGUST**

Whatever things you ask when you pray, believe that you receive them, and you will have them.

— Mark 11:24 (NKJ)

8 AUGUST

We give thanks to God always for all of you, constantly mentioning you in our prayers, remembering before our God and Father your work of faith and labor of love and steadfastness of hope in our Lord Jesus Christ.
— I Thessalonians 1:2, 3 (ESV)

Etrog (yellow citron) for the Sukkot holiday

Jerash, Jordan

9 AUGUST

Walk in love, as Christ loved us and gave Himself up for us, a fragrant offering and sacrifice to God.

— *Ephesians 5:2 (ESV)*

Cotton farm, Israel

10 AUGUST

This is how God showed His love among us: He sent His one and only Son into the world that we might live through Him.

— *1 John 4:9 (NIV)*

Black Canyon, Eilat, Israel

11 AUGUST

These things I have spoken to you, that My joy may remain in you, and that your joy may be full.

— John 15:11 (NKJ)

Ladiko Bay, Rhodes, Greece

12 AUGUST

I press on toward the goal for the prize of the upward call of God in Christ Jesus.

— *Philippians 3:14 (ESV)*

Santorini, Greece

13 AUGUST

Render therefore unto Cesar the things which be Cesar's; and unto God the things which be God's.

— Matthew 22:21 (KJ)

Darbuka, Old City market, Jerusalem

14 AUGUST

Be strong in the Lord and in the strength of His might.
— *Ephesians 6:10 (ESV)*

Pool of Bethesda, Old City, Jerusalem

15 AUGUST

The Lord is not slow in keeping His promise, as some understand slowness. He is patient with you, not wanting anyone to perish, but everyone to come to repentance.
— II Peter 3:9 (NIV)

16 AUGUST

Ye are my friends, if ye do whatsoever I command you. Henceforth I call you not servants; for the servant knoweth not what his lord doeth; but I have called you friends; for all things that I have heard of my Father I have made known unto you.
— John 15: 14, 15 (KJ)

Ibexes, Negev Desert, Israel

Capo Vaticano, Calabria, Italy

17 AUGUST

I will not leave you comfortless; I will come to you.

— John 14:18 (KJ)

Tomb of King David, Mount Zion, Jerusalem

18 AUGUST

As the Father loved Me, I also have loved you; abide in My love.
— *John 15:9 (NKJ)*

Goat pen, Anata, Jerusalem

19 AUGUST

Let the little children come to Me, and do not forbid them; for of such is the kingdom of God.

— Luke 18:16 (NKJ)

Petra, Jordan

20 AUGUST

Peace be unto you; as my Father hath sent me, even so I send you.
— John 20:21 (KJ)

Olive oil press millstone, Capernaum, Israel

21 AUGUST

Whoever sows sparingly will also reap sparingly, and whoever sows bountifully will also reap bountifully.

— II Corinthians 9:6 (ESV)

Kato Galatas, Crete, Greece

22 AUGUST

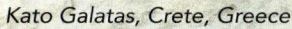

This is what He promised us—even eternal life.

— I John 2:25 (NIV)

Baklava, Carmel Market, TelAviv

23 AUGUST

Blessed are they that mourn: for they shall be comforted.
— Matthew 5:4 (KJ)

24 AUGUST

May our Lord Jesus Christ Himself, and God our Father, who loved us and gave us eternal comfort and good hope through grace, comfort your hearts and establish them in every good work and word.
— *II Thessalonians 2:16, 17*
(ESV)

Basilica entrance, Philippi, Greece

Dead Sea, Israel

25 AUGUST

We know that all things work together for good to those who love God, to those who are the called according to His purpose.

— *Romans 8:28 (NKJ)*

Apollonia National Park, Israel

26 AUGUST

God sent not His Son into the world to condemn the world; but that the world through Him might be saved.

— John 3:17 (KJ)

Bet Mercurios Church, Lalibela, Ethiopia

27 AUGUST

This is love: not that we loved God, but that He loved us and sent His Son as an atoning sacrifice for our sins.

— I John 4:10 (NIV)

28 AUGUST

Corinthians, Greek manuscript on papyrus

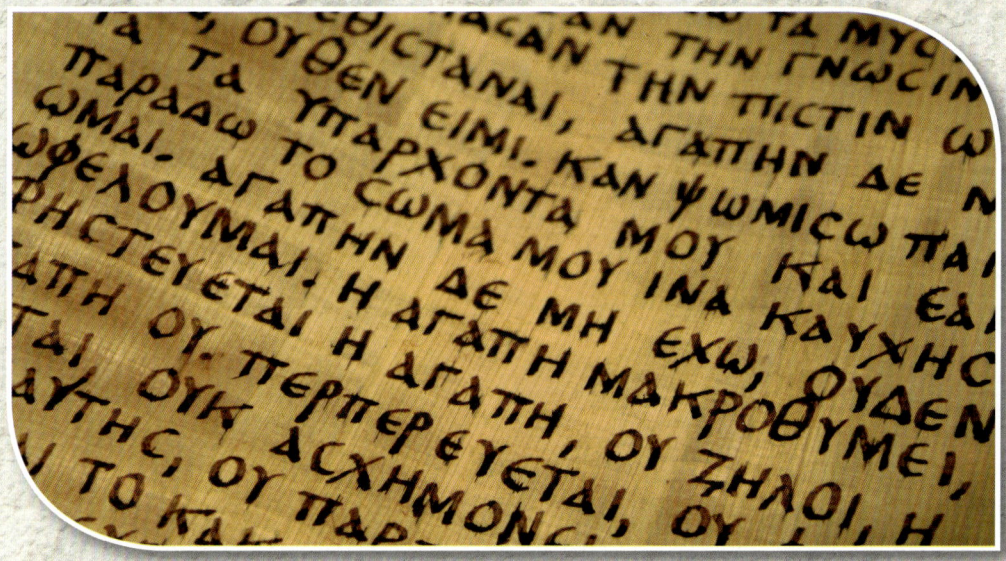

Finally, brothers, rejoice. Aim for restoration, comfort one another, agree with one another, live in peace; and the God of love and peace will be with you.
— II Corinthians 13:11 (ESV)

Fluted giant clam, Red Sea

29 AUGUST

Whatsoever ye shall ask the Father in my name, He will give it you. Hitherto have ye asked nothing in my name: ask, and ye shall receive, that your joy may be full. — *John 16:23, 24 (KJ)*

Jerusalem 30 AUGUST

If we live by the Spirit, let us also walk by the Spirit.
— Galatians 5:25 (ESV)

Ashkelon, Israel

31 AUGUST

If anyone is in Christ, he is a new creation. The old has passed away; behold, the new has come.

— II Corinthians 5:17 (ESV)

1 SEPTEMBER

If two of you agree on earth concerning anything that they ask, it will be done for them by My Father in heaven. For where two or three are gathered together in My name, I am there in the midst of them.
— *Matthew 18:19, 20 (NKJ)*

Thessaloniki, Greece

Jerash, Jordan

2 SEPTEMBER

Blessed are those who have not seen and yet have believed.
— John 20:29 (NKJ)

Frankincense

3 SEPTEMBER

To him who overcomes, I will give the right to sit with me on my throne, just as I overcame and sat down with my Father on His throne.

— *Revelations 3:21 (NIV)*

Galilee mountains, Israel

4 SEPTEMBER

Many are called, but few are chosen.

— Matthew 22:14 (KJ)

St. Bartholomew's Church, Bavaria, Germany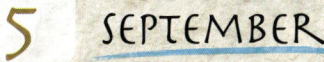

Dear friends, since God so loved us, we also ought to love one another.

— I John 4:11 (NIV)

Tabgha, Israel

6 SEPTEMBER

All of you, live in harmony with one another; be sympathetic, love as brothers, be compassionate and humble.

— I Peter 3:8 (NIV)

7 SEPTEMBER

The Spirit of the Lord is upon me, because He hath anointed me to preach the gospel to the poor; He hath sent me to heal the broken-hearted, to preach deliverance to the captives, and recovering of sight to the blind, to set at liberty them that are bruised.

— *Luke 4:18 (KJ)*

Neda Waterfall, Kyparissia, Greece

Eilat Mountains, Israel

8 SEPTEMBER

I go to prepare a place for you. And if I go and prepare a place for you, I will come again, and receive you unto myself; that where I am, there ye may be also.

— John 14:2, 3 (KJ)

Crusaders' Harbor, Acre, Israel

9 SEPTEMBER

Here I am! I stand at the door and knock. If anyone hears my voice and opens the door, I will come in and eat with him, and he with me.
— *Revelations 3:20 (NIV)*

Roman amphitheater, Caesarea Maritima, Israel — **10 SEPTEMBER**

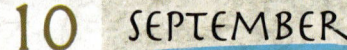

Go into all the world and preach the gospel to every creature.
— Mark 16:15 (NKJ)

Agriculture valley, Galilee, Israel

11 SEPTEMBER

Peace I leave with you, my peace I give unto you: not as the world giveth, give I unto you. Let not your heart be troubled, neither let it be afraid.
— John 14:27 (KJ)

Rosh HaNikra, Galilee, Israel

12 SEPTEMBER

To him who overcomes, I will give the right to eat from the tree of life, which is in the paradise of God.

— *Revelations 2:7 (NIV)*

Oil lamp

13 SEPTEMBER

Love does no harm to a neighbor; therefore love is the fulfilment of the law.

— Romans 13:10 (NKJ)

Temple mount, Jerusalem

14 SEPTEMBER

If you keep My commandments, you will abide in My love, just as I have kept My Father's commandments and abide in His love.

— John 15:10 (NKJ)

15 SEPTEMBER

Let us fix our eyes on Jesus, the author and perfecter of our faith, who for the joy set before Him endured the cross, scorning its shame, and sat down at the right hand of the throne of God.

— Hebrews 12:2 (NIV)

Gulf of Eilat, Red Sea, Israel

Church of St. Paul, Thessaloniki, Greece

16 SEPTEMBER

Brothers, I do not consider that I have made it my own. But one thing I do: forgetting what lies behind and straining forward to what lies ahead.
— Philippians 3:13 (ESV)

Dead Sea, Israel

17 SEPTEMBER

Repay no one evil for evil. Have regard for good things in the sight of all men.

— Romans 12:17 (NKJ)

Ricotia Brassicaceae, Makhtesh Ramon, Negev Desert   18   SEPTEMBER

Come ye yourselves apart into a desert place, and rest a while.
— Mark 6:31 (KJ)

Pigion's Rock, Beirut, Lebanon

19 SEPTEMBER

Present your bodies a living sacrifice, holy, acceptable to God, which is your reasonable service.

— *Romans 12:1 (NKJ)*

Dead Sea, Ein Gedi, Israel

20 SEPTEMBER

For by grace you have been saved through faith. And this is not your own doing; it is the gift of God, not a result of works, so that no one may boast.
— *Ephesians 2:8, 9 (ESV)*

Chapel of the Milk Grotto, Bethlehem, Palestine   **21**   SEPTEMBER

God is a Spirit: and they that worship Him must worship Him in spirit and in truth.

— John 4:24 (KJ)

Red Sea, Israel

22 SEPTEMBER

Whoever does not receive the kingdom of God as a little child will by no means enter it.

— Luke 18:17 (NKJ)

23 SEPTEMBER

For I say, through the grace given to me, to everyone who is among you, not to think of himself more highly than he ought to think, but to think soberly, as God has dealt to each one a measure of faith.
— *Romans 12:3 (NKJ)*

Philippi ruins, Krinides, Greece

Olive trees, Garden of Gethsemane, Jerusalem

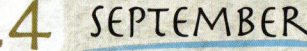
24 SEPTEMBER

All things should be done decently and in order.
— I Corinthians 14:40 (ESV)

Azure Window, Gozo island, Malta

25 SEPTEMBER

He has given us this command: Whoever loves God must also love his brother.

— 1 John 4:21 (NIV)

Dead Sea, Israel

26 SEPTEMBER

It is done. I am the Alpha and the Omega, the Beginning and the End. To him who is thirsty I will give to drink without cost from the spring of the water of life.
— *Revelations 21:6 (NIV)*

Tropea, Calabria, Italy

27 SEPTEMBER

If we know that He hears us--whatever we ask--we know that we have what we asked of Him.

— I John 5:15 (NIV)

Synagogue, Capernaum National Park, Israel

28 SEPTEMBER

If we walk in the light, as He is in the light, we have fellowship with one another, and the blood of Jesus, His Son, purifies us from all sin.

— I John 1:7 (NIV)

Ayia Napa, Cyprus

29 SEPTEMBER

If anyone acknowledges that Jesus is the Son of God, God lives in him and he in God.

— I John 4:15 (NIV)

Fruit Stand, Carmel Market, Tel Aviv

30 SEPTEMBER

To Him who is able to keep you from falling and to present you before His glorious presence without fault and with great joy.

— Jude 1:24 (NIV)

Donkeys, Santorini island, Greece

1 OCTOBER

Blessed are they which do hunger and thirst after righteousness: for they shall be filled.

— *Matthew 5:6 (KJ)*

Our Lady of the Rocks, Bay of Kotor, Montenegro   **2**   OCTOBER

Ye are the salt of the earth: but if the salt have lost his savour, wherewith shall it be salted? It is thenceforth good for nothing, but to be cast out, and to be trodden under foot of men. — *Matthew 5:13 (KJ)*

Beit Guvrin Caves, Ashkelon, Israel

3 OCTOBER

Let all that you do be done in love.

— I Corinthians 16:14 (ESV)

Oia village, Santorini Island, Greece

4 OCTOBER

It is the Spirit who gives life; the flesh profits nothing. The words that I speak to you are spirit, and they are life.

— John 6:63 (NKJ)

Herods Port and Palace ruins, Caesarea Maritima, Israel 5 OCTOBER

All things whatsoever ye would that men should do to you, do ye even so to them: for this is the law and the prophets.

— Matthew 7:12 (KJ)

Camel caravan, Sahara Desert, Morocco

6 OCTOBER

Above all, love each other deeply, because love covers over a multitude of sins.

— I Peter 4:8 (NIV)

Caesarea National Park, Israel

7 OCTOBER

I am coming soon. Hold on to what you have, so that no one will take your crown.

— Revelations 3:11 (NIV)

8 OCTOBER

For I say, through the grace given to me, to everyone who is among you, not to think of himself more highly than he ought to think, but to think soberly, as God has dealt to each one a measure of faith.
— Romans 12:3 (NKJ)

Sinai desert, Egypt

Capernaum, Galilee, Israel — **9 OCTOBER**

Let your light so shine before men, that they may see your good works, and glorify your Father which is in heaven.

— Matthew 5:16 (KJ)

Al-Khazneh ("The Treasury"), Petra, Jordan **10 OCTOBER**

I am sure of this, that He who began a good work in you will bring it to completion at the day of Jesus Christ.

— Philippians 1:6 (ESV)

Dry fruits market stall, Jerusalem, Israel

11 OCTOBER

We love because He first loved us.

— I John 4:19 (NIV)

Hakodate, Japan

12 OCTOBER

He that heareth my word, and believeth on Him that sent me, hath everlasting life, and shall not come into condemnation; but is passed from death unto life. — *John 5:24 (KJ)*

Lionfish, Red Sea

13 OCTOBER

He will wipe every tear from their eyes. There will be no more death or mourning or crying or pain, for the old order of things has passed away.
— *Revelations 21:4 (NIV)*

Hula Lake Nature Reserve, Hula Valley, Israel

14 OCTOBER

Ask, and it shall be given you; seek, and ye shall find; knock, and it shall be opened unto you: for every one that asketh receiveth; and he that seeketh findeth; and to him that knocketh it shall be opened.

— Matthew 7:7, 8 (KJ)

Herd of sheep, the Mount of Olives, Jerusalem — **15 OCTOBER**

All that the Father gives Me will come to Me, and the one who comes to Me I will by no means cast out.

— John 6:37 (NKJ)

16 OCTOBER

Think not that I am come to destroy the law, or the prophets: I am not come to destroy, but to fulfil. Till heaven and earth pass, one jot or one tittle shall in no wise pass from the law, till all be fulfilled.
— *Matthew 5:17, 18 (KJ)*

The Siq, Petra, Jordan

The Tree of Life, Hisham's Palace, Jericho

17 OCTOBER

Complete my joy by being of the same mind, having the same love, being in full accord and of one mind.

— *Philippians 2:2 (ESV)*

Crete, Greece **18 OCTOBER**

Whoever exalts himself will be humbled, and he who humbles himself will be exalted.

— Luke 14:11 (NKJ)

Arbel Cliff National Park, Israel

19 OCTOBER

I will have mercy, and not sacrifice, for I am not come to call the righteous, but sinners to repentance.

— Matthew 9:13 (KJ)

Caesaria, Israel

20 OCTOBER

But thanks be to God, who gives us the victory through our Lord Jesus Christ.

— *I Corinthians 15:57 (ESV)*

Myrrh tree, Yemen

21 OCTOBER

Do not labor for the food which perishes, but for the food which endures to everlasting life, which the Son of Man will give you, because God the Father has set His seal on Him. — *John 6:27 (NKJ)*

Flowers farm, Galilee, Israel

22 OCTOBER

Freely ye have received, freely give.

— Matthew 10:8 (KJ)

Sea of Galilee, Tiberias, Israel | 23 OCTOBER

Dear friends, do not be surprised at the painful trial you are suffering, as though something strange were happening to you.
— I Peter 4:12 (NIV)

24 OCTOBER

Though you have not seen Him, you love Him; and even though you do not see Him now, you believe in Him and are filled with an inexpressible and glorious joy.

— I Peter 1:8 (NIV)

Stone water well, Shiloh, Israel

Roman baths, Corinth, Greece — **25 OCTOBER**

This light momentary affliction is preparing for us an eternal weight of glory beyond all comparison.

— II Corinthians 4:17 (ESV)

Black Canyon, Israel

26 OCTOBER

Assuredly, I say to you, unless you are converted and become as little children, you will by no means enter the kingdom of heaven.

— *Matthew 18:3 (NKJ)*

Almond tree, Sataf Nature Reserve, Israel

27 OCTOBER

It is God who works in you, both to will and to work for His good pleasure.

— *Philippians 2:13 (ESV)*

Chapel of Panagia Kakaviotisa, Lemnos, Greece

28 OCTOBER

I still have many things to say to you, but you cannot bear them now. When He, the Spirit of truth, has come, He will guide you into all truth.
— *John 16:12, 13 (NKJ)*

Hula Nature Reserve, Galilee, Israel

29 OCTOBER

Blessed are the merciful: for they shall obtain mercy.

— Matthew 5:7 (KJ)

Olive Grove, Galilee, Israel

30 OCTOBER

If we confess our sins, He is faithful and just and will forgive us our sins and purify us from all unrighteousness.

— I John 1:9 (NIV)

Mujib Nature Reserve, Dead Sea, Jordan

31 OCTOBER

Give to every man that asketh of thee; and of him that taketh away thy goods ask them not again.

— Luke 6:30 (KJ)

1 NOVEMBER

Enter ye in at the strait gate: for wide is the gate, and broad is the way, that leadeth to destruction, and many there be which go in there at: because strait is the gate, and narrow is the way, which leadeth unto life, and few there be that find it.
— Matthew 7:13, 14 (KJ)

Old fountain's Hebrew inscription "For I will pour water on him who is thirsty", Jaffa, Israel

Halva, Carmel Market, Tel Aviv

2 NOVEMBER

Most assuredly, I say to you, he who believes in Me has everlasting life.

— John 6:47 (NKJ)

Wadi Rum, Jordan

3 NOVEMBER

This is the message we have heard from Him and declare to you: God is light; in Him there is no darkness at all.

— I John 1:5 (NIV)

Deir Mar Takla, Maalula, Syria

4 NOVEMBER

I am the way, the truth, and the life: no man cometh unto the Father, but by me.

— John 14:6 (KJ)

Chellah Kasbah, Morocco

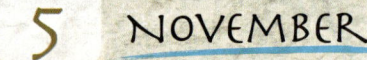
5 NOVEMBER

Can the blind lead the blind? Shall they not both fall into the ditch?
— Luke 6: 39 (KJ)

6 NOVEMBER

You are a chosen people, a royal priesthood, a holy nation, a people belonging to God, that you may declare the praises of Him who called you out of darkness into His wonderful light.

— *I Peter 2:9 (NIV)*

Colored Canyon, Sinai, Egypt

Bat Yam, Israel

7 NOVEMBER

Rejoice that you participate in the sufferings of Christ, so that you may be overjoyed when His glory is revealed.

— I Peter 4:13 (NIV)

Tarsus Waterfall, Turkey — **8 NOVEMBER**

Take heed that ye do not your alms before men, to be seen of them; otherwise ye have no reward of your Father which is in heaven.

— Matthew 6:1 (KJ)

White Tower of Thessaloniki, Greece

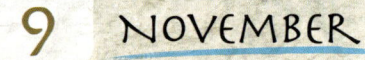

9 NOVEMBER

Blessed are your eyes, for they see: and your ears, for they hear.
— Matthew 13:16 (KJ)

Pomegranate orchard, Jerusalem, Israel

10 NOVEMBER

If anyone keeps My word he shall never see death.

— John 8:51 (NKJ)

Madaba Mosaic Map, Madaba, Jordan

11 NOVEMBER

You are already clean because of the word which I have spoken to you.
— *John 15:3 (NKJ)*

Samothrace Beach, Greece

12 NOVEMBER

Take my yoke upon you, and learn of me; for I am meek and lowly in heart: and ye shall find rest unto your souls. For my yoke is easy, and my burden is light.
— *Matthew 11:29, 30 (KJ)*

Historic water well, Sharon plain, Israel

13 NOVEMBER

To the only God our Savior be glory, majesty, power and authority, through Jesus Christ our Lord, before all ages, now and forevermore! Amen.
— *Jude 1:25 (NIV)*

14 NOVEMBER

Love ye your enemies, and do good, and lend, hoping for nothing again; and your reward shall be great, and ye shall be the children of the Highest: for He is kind unto the unthankful and to the evil. Be ye therefore merciful, as your Father also is.

— Luke 6: 35, 36 (KJ)

Meze, kebab, falafel, baba ghanoush, muhammara, hummus, sambusak, rice, tahini, kibbeh, pita.

Red Poppies and Nazareth Iris, Nazareth, Israel   **15**   NOVEMBER

Whosoever drinketh of the water that I shall give him shall never thirst; but the water that I shall give him shall be in him a well of water springing up into everlasting life.

— *John 4:14 (KJ)*

Palmyra, Homs Governorate, Syria

16 NOVEMBER

Come unto me, all ye that labor and are heavy laden, and I will give you rest.

— Matthew 11:28 (KJ)

Sheep grazing, Judean Desert, Israel

17 NOVEMBER

I am the Alpha and the Omega, says the Lord God, who is, and who was, and who is to come, the Almighty.

— *Revelations 1:8 (NIV)*

North Theatre, Jerash, Jordan

18 NOVEMBER

Thy faith hath saved thee; go in peace.

— Luke 7:50 (KJ)

Damascus Gate, Old City, Jerusalem

19 NOVEMBER

Abide in Me, and I in you. As the branch cannot bear fruit of itself, unless it abides in the vine, neither can you, unless you abide in Me.
— John 15:4 (NKJ)

Ein-Avdat, Israel

20 NOVEMBER

Blessed are the pure in heart: for they shall see God.

— Matthew 5:8 (KJ)

Sandstone cliff, Petra, Jordan

21 NOVEMBER

Let us not grow weary of doing good, for in due season we will reap, if we do not give up.

— Galatians 6:9 (ESV)

22 NOVEMBER

Dear friends, now we are children of God, and what we will be has not yet been made known. But we know that when He appears, we shall be like Him, for we shall see Him as He is.

— I John 3:2 (NIV)

The Church of the Primacy of Saint Peter, Tabgha, Israel

Golan Heights, Israel

23 NOVEMBER

Ye are the light of the world. A city that is set on an hill cannot be hid.
— Matthew 5:14 (KJ)

Hasankeyf, Turkey

24 NOVEMBER

He who has My commandments and keeps them, it is he who loves Me. And he who loves Me will be loved by My Father, and I will love him and manifest Myself to him.
— John 14:21 (NKJ)

Pamukkale, Denizli Province, Turkey

25 NOVEMBER

Young men, in the same way be submissive to those who are older. All of you, clothe yourselves with humility toward one another, because, God opposes the proud but gives grace to the humble. — *I Peter 5:5 (NIV)*

Turkish Delight

26 NOVEMBER

I say to you, do not worry about your life, what you will eat; nor about the body, what you will put on. Life is more than food, and the body is more than clothing. — *Luke 12:22, 23 (NKJ)*

Siq al-Barid, Petra, Jordan

27 NOVEMBER

Blessed is he, whosoever shall not be offended in me.

— Matthew 11:6 (KJ)

Sand Hills of Samaria, Israel

28 NOVEMBER

Be angry and do not sin; do not let the sun go down on your anger.
— Ephesians 4:26 (ESV)

Aish baladi, Egyptian flatbread

29 NOVEMBER

Give us this day our daily bread.

— Matthew 6:11 (KJ)

Mar Saba, Bethlehem, Palestine

30 NOVEMBER

As ye would that men should do to you, do ye also to them likewise.
— Luke 6:31 (KJ)

St Finbarr's Oratory, Cork, Ireland

1 DECEMBER

Be steadfast, immovable, always abounding in the work of the Lord, knowing that in the Lord your labor is not in vain.
— *I Corinthians 15:58 (ESV)*

Fishing boat, Sea of Galilee, Israel

2 DECEMBER

Rejoice, and be exceeding glad: for great is your reward in heaven: for so persecuted they the prophets which were before you.

— Matthew 5:12 (KJ)

Vineyard, Kfar Tabor, Israel

3 DECEMBER

If anyone thirsts, let him come to Me and drink. He who believes in Me, as the Scripture has said, out of his heart will flow rivers of living water.
— *John 7:37, 38 (NKJ)*

Soreq Avshalom Cave, Israel

4 DECEMBER

Now the Lord is the Spirit, and where the Spirit of the Lord is, there is freedom.

— II Corinthians 3:17 (ESV)

Meteora, Greece

5 DECEMBER

For the Lamb at the center of the throne will be their shepherd; he will lead them to springs of living water. And God will wipe away every tear from their eyes.
— *Revelations 7:17 (NIV)*

Mount Hermon, Israel   **6**   DECEMBER

If ye forgive men their trespasses, your heavenly Father will also forgive you: but if ye forgive not men their trespasses, neither will your Father forgive your trespasses.
— Matthew 6:14, 15 (KJ)

7 DECEMBER

Give, and it shall be given unto you; good measure, pressed down, and shaken together, and running over, shall men give into your bosom. For with the same measure that ye mete withal it shall be measured to you again.
— *Luke 6:38 (KJ)*

Church of the Beatitudes, Tabgha, Israel

Spinner dolphins (Stenella longirostris), Red Sea, Egypt — 8 DECEMBER

Cast all your anxiety on Him because He cares for you.
— I Peter 5:7 (NIV)

Spice stall, The Shuk, Jerusalem

9 DECEMBER

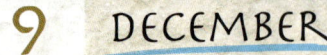

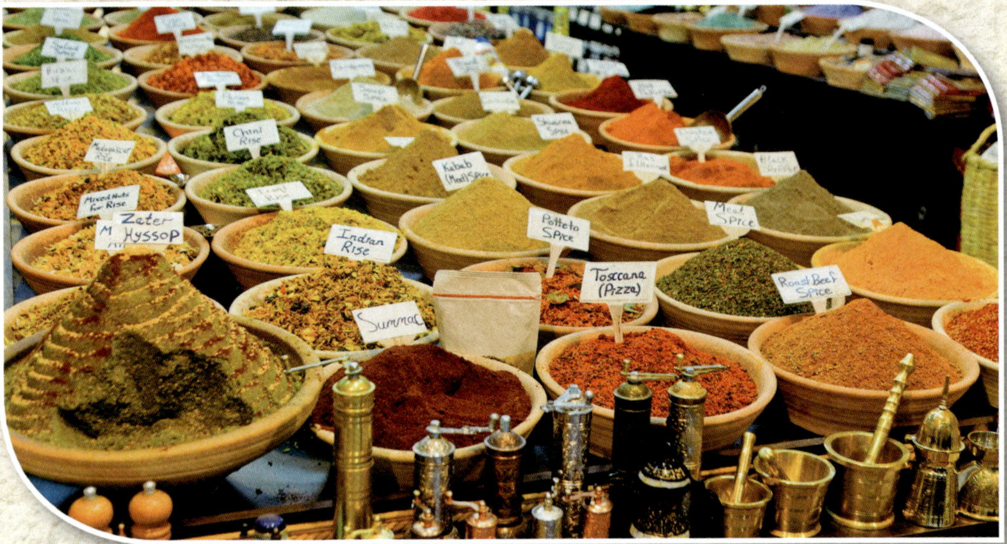

I have no greater joy than to hear that my children are walking in the truth.

— III John 1:4 (NIV)

Kafr Kanna, Israel

10 DECEMBER

There is no fear in love. But perfect love drives out fear, because fear has to do with punishment. The one who fears is not made perfect in love.

— I John 4:18 (NIV)

Purple Heron, Sea of Galilee, Israel

11 DECEMBER

I am the good shepherd; and I know My sheep, and am known by My own, and I lay down My life for the sheep.

— John 10:14, 15 (NKJ)

St. Peters fish (Tilapia), pilgrims's meal, Sea of Galilee 12 DECEMBER

Do not fear, little flock, for it is your Father's good pleasure to give you the kingdom.

— Luke 12:32 (NKJ)

Gethsemane Olive Orchard, Mount of Olives, Jerusalem   **13**   DECEMBER

Bear one another's burdens, and so fulfill the law of Christ.
— Galatians 6:2 (ESV)

Almond grove, Latrun, Israel

14 DECEMBER

Judge not, that ye be not judged. For with what judgment ye judge, ye shall be judged: and with what measure ye mete, it shall be measured to you again.
— Matthew 7:1, 2 (KJ)

15 DECEMBER

I know your deeds. See, I have placed before you an open door that no one can shut. I know that you have little strength, yet you have kept my word and have not denied my name.
— *Revelations 3:8 (NIV)*

Crete, Greece

Rion-Antirion Bridge, Gulf of Corinth, Greece   16   DECEMBER

I will pray the Father, and He shall give you another Comforter, that He may abide with you for ever; even the Spirit of truth…for He dwelleth with you, and shall be in you.   — *John 14:16, 17 (KJ)*

Tzabar cactus, Negev desert, Israel

17 DECEMBER

Take therefore no thought for the morrow: for the morrow shall take thought for the things of itself. Sufficient unto the day is the evil thereof.
— Matthew 6:34 (KJ)

Red Sea, Egypt

18 DECEMBER

For though we walk in the flesh, we are not waging war according to the flesh.

— II Corinthians 10:3 (ESV)

Basilica of St. Paul, Harissa, Lebanon

19 DECEMBER

Each one must give as he has decided in his heart, not reluctantly or under compulsion, for God loves a cheerful giver.

— II Corinthians 9:7 (ESV)

Petra, Jordan

20 DECEMBER

Lay not up for yourselves treasures upon earth, where moth and rust doth corrupt. For where your treasure is, there will your heart be also.

— *Matthew 6:19 (KJ)*

Nile river, Aswan, Egypt

21 DECEMBER

Do not judge according to appearance, but judge with righteous judgment.

— John 7:24 (NKJ)

22 December

Again, the kingdom of heaven is like a dragnet that was cast into the sea and gathered some of every kind, which, when it was full, they drew to shore; and they sat down and gathered the good into vessels, but threw the bad away.
— *Matthew 13:47, 48 (NKJ)*

Turkish coffee and pistachio halva

Jerusalem Bagels, Old City, Jerusalem

23 DECEMBER

Keep yourselves in God's love as you wait for the mercy of our Lord Jesus Christ to bring you to eternal life.

— Jude 1:21 (NIV)

Cappadocia, Anatolia, Turkey

24 DECEMBER

We look not to the things that are seen but to the things that are unseen. For the things that are seen are transient, but the things that are unseen are eternal.

— *II Corinthians 4:18 (ESV)*

Chapel, Allgäu, Germany

25 DECEMBER

Blessed are the peacemakers: for they shall be called the children of God.

— *Matthew 5:9 (KJ)*

Saint Catherine's Monastery, Sinai, Egypt — **26 DECEMBER**

Blessed are those who hear the word of God and keep it!

— Luke 11:28 (NKJ)

Sinai Peninsula, Egypt

27 DECEMBER

This is how we know what love is: Jesus Christ laid down His life for us. And we ought to lay down our lives for our brothers.

— I John 3:16 (NIV)

Royal Park Montazah, Alexandria. Egypt 28 DECEMBER

Forgive us our debts, as we forgive our debtors.

— Matthew 6:12 (KJ)

Dahab, Egypt

29 DECEMBER

I am the door. If anyone enters by Me, he will be saved, and will go in and out and find pasture.

— John 10:9 (NKJ)

Vegetable stall, Tel Aviv, Israel

30 DECEMBER

Dear friends, let us love one another, for love comes from God. Everyone who loves has been born of God and knows God.

— I John 4:7 (NIV)

31 DECEMBER

In your hearts set apart Christ as Lord. Always be prepared to give an answer to everyone who asks you to give the reason for the hope that you have. But do this with gentleness and respect.

— I Peter 3:15 (NIV)

Palestine Sunbird